YOU CAN DO IT
GUIDE TO SCHOOL SUCCESS

by Rebecca Allen

illustrated by Estella Hickman

Published by Worthington Press
7099 Huntley Road, Worthington, Ohio 43085

Copyright © 1989 by Worthington Press

All rights reserved. No portion of this book may be reproduced, stored in a retrieval system, or transmitted, in any form or by any means, electronic, mechanical, photocopying, recording, or otherwise without prior written permission from the publisher.

Printed in the United States of America
10 9 8 7 6 5 4 3 2 1

ISBN 0-87406-414-7

*To my parents,
Catherine and Robert Zimmerman—
for always believing in me*

Contents

1. **School Success—What Is It? 7**
   Defining Success for You 10
   Setting Your Own Goals 19
   Taking Responsibility 27

2. **Success With Grades 33**
   Getting the Most Out of Class 34
   Improving Your Study Skills 44
   Tips on Taking a Test 56
   Rules for Better Writing 59

3. **Success With Friends 67**
   Being Yourself With Friends 68
   Getting Along With Friends 74
   Keeping Your Friends 80
   Making New Friends 83

4. **Success With Extracurricular Activities 89**
   Deciding What's Right for You 92
   So You're Not a Star 98
   Getting Along With a Group 101
   Making the Most of Your
   Extracurricular Activities 108

5. **Achieving Balance** 111
   Know Your Own Limits 113
   Set Priorities 118
   Be More Efficient 120
   Battle Stress 123

1

What is school success? How would you define it? A dictionary defines success as "reaching a desired end or goal." The key word in this definition is *desired*. Success in anything—a job, a sport, a class—means reaching a goal that you desire, not one that's important to your best friend or your older sister. Success means reaching a goal that's important to you.

If you asked every student in your school what school success means to them, you would probably get hundreds of different answers. That's because the question really means "What are *your* standards of school success? What would it take to make *you* feel successful in school?"

For a student who has always been afraid of speaking in front of an audience, getting even a small part in the school play might mean success. For someone who has never done well in sports, joining the track team might make a difference. For a student who has always failed math, earning a C might be the desired goal.

Success means

something different to each person. And whatever success is—it's not hard to recognize! There's nothing quite like that wonderful, tingly feeling that comes from being successful.

So, dig in! You'll find success, too. There's no doubt about it! The *You Can Do It Guide to School Success* will help you decide what school success means to you, as well as how to achieve it. This book will show you how to make friendships, extracurricular activities, and grades work for you. The key to making life at school a lot more enjoyable is *balancing your commitments*.

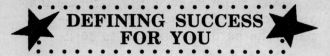

DEFINING SUCCESS FOR YOU

It's not hard to find out what school success means to other people. They're usually happy to tell you. Your parents may tell you how important it is to earn all *A*s and *B*s. Your sister may tell you that school success means having lots of friends. The coach may tell you that being on a winning team is what counts most.

It's hard to figure out what success means to you when you're constantly bombarded by other people's ideas of success. Even though there is nothing wrong with wanting to earn other people's respect, you can't let them define what success means to you.

Okay, so far so good. But agreeing that you need to define your success is the easy part. The hard part is *how* to do it!

To start with, you need to know three main characteristics of yourself. You need to know what your *skills*, your *interests*, and your *values* are. Why do you need to know these things? Because then you can try activities that you are good at, ones you enjoy, or ones that are important to you.

Look at it this way. No one can succeed at everything. So, why not go after those things that are especially suited to you! What do you think Michael Jackson's friends would say to him if he woke up one morning and said, "I think I'll give up singing and dancing and become a world-class chess player"? Or, what if Joe Montana decided that he was tired of winning Super Bowls and wanted to open a shoe-repair shop? Wouldn't their friends say, "Look, guys. Stick to what you do best!"

To find out what *you* do best, look closely at your *skills*, *interests*, and *values*.

▶ Your Skills

Without a good understanding of your skills and abilities, you may develop unrealistic expectations for yourself. For instance, you may set a goal of being a track star. But if you've never even been on a sports team before, becoming a track star may be a very difficult goal to attain. Or, maybe you decide that your school success depends on playing first violin in the school orchestra. But if you're just a beginner on the violin, you may be in for a big shock when you realize how hard it is to play the fiddle! And if you've always gotten *D*s in math, do you think it would be a realistic goal to try to get only *A*s?

Let's face it. Not everyone is an athlete, a musician, or a math whiz. But every person does have certain strengths and weaknesses. Know what yours are! Then set realistic goals that are appropriate for each area.

A chart like the one below can help you look at your skills and abilities in many different areas. Remember to be honest with yourself!

Strong Skills	Average Skills	Weak Skills
math	playing piano	history
science	writing	art
playing chess	acting	spelling
baseball	speaking	organizing
making friends		carpentry

Now let's consider some realistic goals for each skill listed. With strengths in math and science, this student might set a realistic goal of earning an *A* or *B* in both subjects. He might also decide to enter an experiment in the science fair. And it may be appropriate for this student to join the chess club or try out for the baseball team.

With a weakness in art, though, it would be frustrating for him to expect to win a prize in the school art contest. A better goal might be helping with decorations for a school dance or pep rally. Poor organizational skills would make running for class treasurer pretty difficult. But working in the school cafeteria might be the perfect thing.

There's nothing wrong with challenging yourself. But don't set the stage for defeat. Set realistic goals, not impossible ones. Success doesn't mean being the best at everything. It means feeling good about who you are and what you're doing.

▶ Your Interests

What do you find yourself wanting to do in your spare time? What excites you, makes you happy, or fills you with curiosity? These are your interests. To define what school success means to you, it's important to know what your interests are. Your motivation will be higher for the things you're interested in. Your enthusiasm will be higher, too. That's just the way it is.

Try making a chart like the one below for yourself.

What I do for Fun:
  roller skate, dance, listen to music, be with friends
What I'd Like to Learn About:
  skiing, sailing, astronomy
What Makes Me Feel Good:
  working with wood, drawing, writing poetry

Once your chart is complete, choose three or four interests to pursue at school. This student has lots of options. She could join the ski club, help organize school dances or roller skating parties, enter a poetry contest, or take a wood shop course. Because she has an interest in these areas, she'll probably find both success and enjoyment in pursuing them.

clubs, parties, dances

▶ Your Values

Your values are those things that are important to you. Below is a list of some personal values people have.

making money	helping others
happiness	power
independence	success
fame	being admired
competition	friendships
being alone	change and variety
adventure	excitement
freedom	challenge
opinion of others	good education
responsibility	being creative
good health	

Select five or six of these values (or any others) that are particularly important to you. Then ask yourself "What am I doing to pursue these values? Are there activities at school that can help fulfill my values?"

Let's suppose that you value creativity. There are endless opportunities to be creative at school. You could paint a mural on the cafeteria wall or decorate the gym for a dance. You could play an instrument in the band or start a dance group.

Maybe you value helping others. Use your imagination! You could start a school drive to help the homeless or be a tutor. You could join a community service organization or start one in your school.

If competition is your thing, get into a sport. Choose a team or an individual sport. Or, maybe debating is more your style. There's also chess, spelling, writing, art contests, and about 500

500 TO CHOOSE FROM!

more activities to choose from!

In the same sense, if having a lot of friends isn't something you value, then don't make it one of your priorities. If you get satisfaction from being challenged, then don't settle for the easy jobs. You'll soon become bored and lose interest. Think carefully about what is important to you. Make those things be your goals.

To make the picture even clearer, make a three-column chart that lists your skills or abilities, your main interests, and your most important values. Take a good long look at it. This is the framework for building success into your school experiences.

So, what's next? Let's really set some goals.

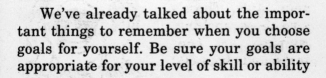

SETTING YOUR OWN GOALS

We've already talked about the important things to remember when you choose goals for yourself. Be sure your goals are appropriate for your level of skill or ability and are especially meaningful and interesting to you. Let's look at how you might choose some goals in three areas of your school life. You could set goals for your *grades*, your *friends*, and your *extracurricular activities*.

▶ **Your Grades**
You're never going to like all the subjects that you take in school equally well. Just accept that. But you'll still end up taking some subjects you just don't feel all that interested in. That's why it's important for your goals in each class to match your ability and level of interest in the subject. And remember that you can't be the best student in *every* subject. You can only be the best you can be.

Let's start by taking a look at where you are now and where you'd like to be by the end of the year. Make a list of all the subjects you're taking this year in school. Rate each subject according to the typical grade you earn. Assign it a four if you usually get *A*s, a three for *B*s, a two for *C*s, and a one for *D*s. Assign no points for a failing grade. Then total the number of points for all your subjects.

Rate each subject according to the grade you'd *like* to get and think maybe you *could* get. Then total those points. How much of a difference is there between your actual total and your desired total? If there is no difference, you don't need to read further. But if there is a difference in total points, that means you'd like to be more successful in a few of your classes. So read on!

Math (C)	2	3
English (B)	3	4
Science (A)	4	4
History (C)	2	2
	11	13

Look at your actual total, and decide how much higher you'd like to raise it by the next grading period. Be conservative in your estimate. What are the subjects in which you could reasonably improve? Raising your total by one or two points is plenty for starters. Remember that goals need to be realistic!

Once you've decided which subjects to concentrate on, think about how you'll achieve a higher grade. Here are some ideas.

➤ *Get extra help after school.*
➤ *Do the homework for that subject first.*
➤ *Spend an extra half hour on that subject.*
➤ *Listen more carefully in class.*

The next chapter will give you a lot more specific ideas on how to improve your grades. But for starters you've got some realistic goals.

Your Friends

Having friends is important to everyone. Some people like to have a lot of friends. Other people prefer to have just one or two close friends. No matter which situation you like, it's important to know how to fit friendships into your life.

There's only one big problem with friends. It's usually a lot more fun to mess around with friends than to practice the piano or study for a big test. So, an important goal to set in school is how and when to fit in time for friends.

You've probably heard the saying "work before pleasure." But have you ever stopped to think what really good advice this is?

Suppose it's a weekend. Your homework is to study for a history test and do three pages of math problems. But your friends want you to go shopping and see a movie with them. What do you do first?

If you're like many students, you spend time with your friends first. But the whole time you're with them, you're dreading the work that's waiting for you at home rather than enjoying yourself. You wait until after supper on Sunday night to tackle your homework. And what happens? You don't have the energy to do the work. In fact, the whole experience feels like torture!

But if you do your homework first, the time with your friends seems like a reward. The work is out of the way, and it's time to have fun. So, "work before pleasure" turns out to be good advice.

"But what if my friends don't understand?" you might ask. "What if they get angry when I say I have to work first?" you wonder.

Well, that could happen. But if you're honest with your friends and explain your reasons, they'll eventually understand. In fact, they'll probably admire your self-discipline. If they're really

your friends, they'll be willing to arrange their free time around yours.

There may be other goals that you'd like to set in the area of friends. Take some time to think about how you'd like to improve your friendships. Here are some possible ways of doing that.

→ *Make some new friends.*
→ *Learn how to be more myself with friends.*
→ *Learn how to say no to my friends.*
→ *Learn how to understand my friends.*
→ *Learn how to accept my friends for who they are.*
→ *Learn how to get along with my friends.*

Chapter three will help you achieve these goals and others. But knowing what your goals are is the first step toward reaching them. Soon, you'll be finding success with friends, too!

▶ Your Extracurricular Activities

No matter what grade you're in, you're probably facing pressures to get involved in school activities. Your friends are joining teams, clubs, and committees all over the school. And with each membership comes a commitment of time and energy. But extracurricular activities have a lot to offer you. You can make new friends, learn new skills, develop new interests, and have a lot of fun in the process.

You may already know which extracurricular activities you'd like to join. But squeezing them into an already packed schedule is another thing. Whatever you do, don't be tempted to join too many activities at once. It's always best to try one activity at a time to see if you like it and can fit it into your schedule. Be sure you understand how much of a time and energy commitment you're making.

If you're confused about which activities would be best for you, here are some questions you can ask yourself.

⟶ *What do I want to gain from the activity?*
⟶ *Do other members have goals similar to mine?*
⟶ *Can I afford the time and effort required by the activity?*
⟶ *Is the activity something I'll be good at, enjoy, or find valuable?*

Finding the answers to these questions should help you select the best extracurricular activities for you. Chapter four has even more advice about extracurricular activities.

★ TAKING RESPONSIBILITY ★

Now that you've set some goals, you need to take responsibility for achieving them. You know where you want to be. Now dig in, and get there!

Here are a few tips to get you started.

1 *Divide your major goals into smaller ones.* You've chosen the goal to earn a *B* in history. Here are some lesser goals you might need to achieve first.

→ Read each chapter when it's assigned.
→ Turn in all assigned homework.
→ Earn a *B* average on all quizzes.
→ Earn a *B* on the unit test.

To reach each of these goals, break them down still further. For instance, suppose your goal one week is to earn a *B* on the chapter quiz. What do you need to do? And when do you plan to do it? Make a schedule for yourself several days before the quiz.

Monday: Read over chapter subheadings, boldface print, and captions. Look at chapter summary.
Tuesday: Read over class notes. Highlight important information.
Wednesday: Memorize important facts and details.
Thursday: Look over notes during lunch. Take quiz.

2 *Establish your priorities.* It's a good idea to do this daily. Make a list of everything you need to do for the day. Then number it. The number one item should be the first thing you want to do. Then move down your list in order. Save the fun things for last. Then you'll be free to enjoy them. Do the hardest things first. Once you complete a task, cross it off your list by making a big dark mark through it. You'll feel a great sense of accomplishment!

3 *Don't procrastinate.* It's so easy to wait until the last minute to start a chore you don't really want to do. But the whole time you put it off, you worry about getting it done.

If you know a week in advance that a test is coming up or a paper is due, start working on it immediately. Even if you just glance at chapter headings or jot down ideas to write about, it's a start. Accomplishing even the smallest amount of work gives you the motivation to go on.

The next time you get a long-term assignment, remember the last time you procrastinated. It wasn't a very good feeling cramming all the work into the last day, was it?

4 *Don't count on others to do it for you.* If you lead the busy life that most students do, you might feel more organized using a pocket calendar. In it you can write due dates for homework assignments, chores you have promised to complete, dates you've made with friends, times for club meetings, or birthdays you don't want to forget. Don't expect other people to remind you of these things. They're busy enough with their own lives! Learning to manage your own affairs is a skill that will make your whole life a lot easier.

Well, you're off to a good start! You've thought about what school success means to you. You've set some goals. And you're ready to take full responsibility for meeting those goals. The chapters ahead will carry you further along the road to school success.

2

If you think that getting good grades is tough, just think about the alternative. Getting bad grades is a whole lot harder! How would it feel to always be the last to turn in your papers, to never know the answer when the teacher calls on you, or to always hang your head when you show your parents another report card?

Finding success with grades is something you'll be proud of. Not only will you gain knowledge, you'll gain a whole list of valuable skills. And best of all, you'll gain confidence in knowing that you did it all yourself.

So, if you're ready to get started, read on. You'll learn how to get the most out of class, improve your study skills, take tests, and write better papers.

★ GETTING THE MOST OUT OF CLASS ★

▶ **Really Being There**

To really get the most out of any class, you've got to *be there*—physically and mentally. If you don't give your best effort in class, you're behind before you even begin.

To be in class physically means getting

off to school on time. And that means planning your morning carefully. It may help to write out a schedule so you don't get behind. Consider when you have to be at your first class, and work backward. Be sure to account for the time you need to go to your locker, to talk to friends, to travel to school, to make your lunch, to eat breakfast, and to get dressed. Be generous in your estimate. There's nothing worse than rushing around early in the morning.

To save time, try setting out your clothes and packing your books in your book bag the night before. Decide when to get up, and set your alarm. If you find that you're not getting enough sleep, go to bed earlier. You should be getting at least eight hours of sleep each night. You won't get the most out of class if you're nodding off to sleep when the teacher is talking.

Part of being in class physically is being prepared. And that requires certain tools.

1 *Make an assignment book.* Try a small pad of paper or a notebook for keeping track of homework assignments. If it's arranged like a calendar, you can write in due dates for assignments, as well as other responsibilities and important dates.

2 *Carry plenty of pens, pencils, erasers.* It's easy to lose track of these. Try keeping them in a zippered plastic bag.

3 *Find some folders.* A good way to organize handouts is with pocket folders. You can buy folders that fit in a three-ring notebook or ones that stand alone. You can even buy folders to match the color of the spiral notebook you have for each class.

4 *Wear a watch.* Make it a habit to wear a wristwatch. It will help you manage your time better and get to class on time.

5 *Choose a notebook.* You can use a three-ring notebook with dividers for each subject, or you might prefer a small spiral notebook for each class.

6 *Carry a backpack or book bag.* It's a lot easier to carry all your school supplies in something. You're less likely to lose a whole bag than you are a small pencil or notebook.

Being in class mentally has a lot to do with how you're feeling physically. It's pretty hard to pay attention when you feel sick or uncomfortable. If you feel miserable, stay home, and get well. Taking care of yourself will shorten your sick time.

If you feel uncomfortable in your seat, get up, and move around without disturbing others. Shift in your seat, or tighten and then relax different parts of your body. This will increase your circulation and make you feel refreshed.

It's hard to be in class mentally if you have your mind on other things. If a thought that you want to remember enters your mind, jot it down in a notebook. Then try to forget it until later. When personal problems come up, try to deal with them as soon as possible. Don't let them drag on, or they'll drag you down. Talk with your friends or your parents if you need some help. And don't forget about the school counselors. They're specially trained to help students with all kinds of problems.

▶ Learning How to Listen

Learning how to listen will also help you get the most out of class. Here are some ways to improve your listening skills.

1 *Sit in the front.* If possible, choose a seat near the front of the class. You'll feel more involved in what the teacher is saying. Watch the teacher closely. This will help you listen better.

2 *Keep alert.* To keep your mind alert, take a deep breath every few minutes. Stretch a muscle or two. Glance out the window. Concentrating for too long can tire you out.

3 *Concentrate.* Focus on what the teacher is saying. Get actively involved in listening. Ask yourself what point the teacher is trying to make? Organize the information you're hearing in your mind. How do all the details fit together? What are the main points? Try to form a mental picture of what's being said. This will help you understand the material better.

▶ Taking Good Notes

In classes where teachers lecture a lot, note-taking skills are a must. Good notes help you remember what the teacher thinks is important. Good notes help you learn the subject, prepare for the next day's class, and do well on tests. To take good notes, remember these simple rules.

1 *Listen to opening lines.* Teachers usually begin their lectures by telling you what they're going to say. If your teacher begins by saying, "Today we're going to talk about the circulatory system." Write this down, and keep it in mind as you listen.

2 *Listen for key phrases.* These phrases indicate important information. "The purpose of this," "The main idea," "The conclusion of the story," "The end product," and "The value of this" are all key phrases that indicate that you should take notes on what your teacher is going to say next.

3 *Listen to connecting phrases.* Phrases like "First of all," "Secondly," "Furthermore," "On the other hand," "Consequently," "For example," and others indicate that the teacher is filling in the details of the lecture. She may be listing details, giving examples, or offering comparisons. This information is always worth jotting down.

4 *Use the note form that works best for you.* You may prefer using the outline form. Underline or highlight the main points, and indent the details and examples. Or, draw diagrams by circling the main ideas and drawing lines out from these to indicate supportive information. Draw lines out from these lines to show details and examples.

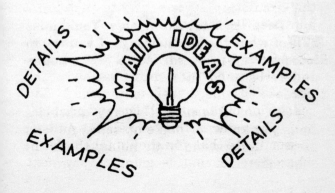

5 *Pay attention to what your teacher thinks is important.* Many teachers will tell you what they think is important to remember. Others may repeat important information in the same words, or they may vary the words. Some teachers will alter the volume or the tone of their voice when giving important information. Pay particular attention to your teacher's gestures. If your teacher suddenly becomes more expressive with his arms and face, he is probably saying something that he wants you to remember.

6 *Write down key words only.* You'll miss half of what the teacher says if you try to jot down every word. Write down nouns and verbs only.

7 *Use abbreviations.* Use any abbreviations you know, or make up some. As long as *you* understand your notes, that's all that matters.

If you have to be absent from class, ask to borrow notes from someone who takes good ones. Offer to return the favor sometime.

▶ **Getting Involved**

Many teachers will expect you to get actively involved in class. Some teachers prefer to do all the talking. Other teachers will expect you to speak up, ask questions, and take part in class discussions. They want you to think for yourself and share your ideas.

For some students, speaking up in class is difficult. If you feel nervous and unsure of yourself, try these tips.

1 *Listen carefully.* Follow the flow of conversation in a discussion. Try building on what others have said. Let the class know if you agree or disagree with what other people have said.

2 *Speak with confidence.* Speak clearly and directly. Don't mumble or act unsure of yourself. What you have to say is worth saying! Don't let others interrupt you.

3 *Be brief.* Keep your comments brief and to the point.

4 *Don't be afraid to ask.* If you don't understand something your teacher or fellow class member has said, ask politely for further explanation. You're probably not the only one who's confused.

★ IMPROVING YOUR STUDY SKILLS ★

The time you spend at home studying is just as important as the time you spend in school. Here are some tips to help you get the most out of your study time.

→ Plan your study time.
→ Plan your study place.
→ Know your learning style.
→ Know your study skills.

▶ Planning Your Study Time

Do you ever feel like you need more hours in the day? To make the most of your time, it's really important to plan out your day. This means writing up a schedule and sticking to it.

Unless you have a study hall during school, you have to study between the time you get home from school and the time you go to bed. This is about six hours a day. But during that time, you also have to eat dinner, do any chores you might have, do some fun stuff, make phone calls, and get ready for bed. How do you fit it all in?

```
Monday
Schedule
DINNER       1 hr.
CHORES       1 hr.
ENGLISH      2 hrs.
MATH         1 hr.
PIANO        30 min.
PHONE CALLS  30 min.
TOTAL        6 hrs.
```

Start by deciding how much time it will take you to do each activity. Be realistic in your estimate. Let's say it will take you an hour to do your math assignment and two hours to write your English composition. That's three hours.

Then look at the other things you'd like to do. You usually spend a half hour practicing piano. You like to talk to your friends for a half hour. Dinner and helping with the dishes takes an hour. It takes an hour to unwind and get ready for bed. Then there's an hour special on TV that you wanted to watch. Oops! That adds up to another four hours! You've overshot your total of six hours. Something has to go!

Look at your time estimates more closely. Are there any ways you can rearrange your schedule? Trying to squeeze three hours of homework into two hours is probably not a good idea. Break some activities into smaller pieces, and assign times to those. Play around with these pieces until you come up with a schedule you can live with. Don't try to schedule every second or forget about having some fun. But you may have to make some

choices. You may have to forget about watching TV or talking to your best friend on the phone.

Here are some hints for making your study time more productive.

1 *Vary your activities.* Studying for three hours straight is hard for anyone. Study for an hour, and then practice your piano. Study for another hour, and then call a friend.

2 *Reward yourself.* Set goals, and reward yourself for achieving them. Tell yourself, "When I've read 10 pages, I'll listen to my stereo for 10 minutes." Or, say, "When I've answered the first 10 questions, I'll make a five-minute phone call to my friend."

3 *Take a break.* Take a five-minute break from your studying every half hour or so. Stretch. Walk around the house.

Do some jumping jacks. Or, walk outside to get some fresh air. You'll feel more alert and be ready to dig in again.

4 *Set limits.* Set limits on the amount of time you'll spend on certain assignments. If you know you have from 5:00 until 6:00 to finish your math problems, you'll be more efficient during the time you're working.

5. *Make studying a habit.* Try studying at exactly the same time each day. If you know that at 6:30 each evening you're going to sit down and study, it becomes more of a habit.

▶ **Planning Your Study Place**

Planning your study place is just as important as planning your study time. Most students find that they need five basic things in their study place. They need a desk, a lamp, a chair, supplies, and QUIET.

6 *Sit at a desk.* If you don't already have a desk, try making your own by placing a smooth board or flat door across cement blocks or wooden crates. There might also be an old desk or table in your basement or attic that you could use. Keep your desk clean and organized. You'll get nowhere if it's cluttered.

7 *Turn on a light.* Any light will do. But avoid a light that's too bright or too dim.

8 *Choose your chair.* Choose a chair that's firm and not so comfortable that you'll fall asleep in it.

9 *Gather your supplies.* Supplies should be close at hand. If you have a desk drawer, use it. If you don't, keep supplies in shoe boxes, silverware trays, or jars on top of your desk. Some supplies you might want to have available are pens and pencils, clock, pencils, a calculator, eraser, ruler or straightedge, paper, stapler, dictionary, paper clips, thesaurus, tape, and scissors.

10 *Find some quiet.* Find a quiet place to work, away from any distractions. If you share a bedroom, try agreeing on a quiet time when you both can study. Or, set up a schedule that allows time for each of you to study alone.

If your bedroom isn't the best place, consider a corner of the attic or basement. If you must study in a noisy spot, try using a mini-stereo with headphones to block out disturbances. Just be sure the music you listen to isn't too distracting.

▶ Knowing Your Learning Style

We all have different learning styles. Do you prefer a cool room or a warm one? Do you work best in a large open space or a small cozy one? Do you study best alone or with friends? Do you do your best work in the morning, afternoon, or evening? Do you study best on an empty stomach or a full one? All of these are factors in your learning style. Try experimenting with different conditions. Maybe you'll discover a better style for you.

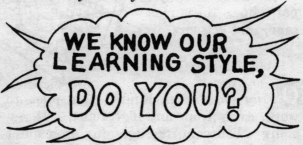

▶ Knowing Your Study Skills

Your homework generally falls into four categories. Your homework activities can include reading textbooks, doing written assignments, studying for tests, and writing papers.

Here are some tips to follow when reading a textbook.

1 *Survey the reading.* Look over your reading assignment from beginning to end. Read headings and subheadings. Look at graphs, charts, diagrams, pictures, and captions. This helps you build a mental map of the assigned pages.

2 *Focus on the main ideas.* Look at the questions at the end of the reading assignment. Look at the chapter preview or summary. These places usually cover the main ideas the author wants you to get. Keep these in mind while you read.

3 *Read section by section.* As you read each section, keep reminding yourself of how each section fits into the whole picture. Stay alert. Read quickly for understanding. Then stop, and ask yourself what you've read.

4 *Underline key points.* You can only do this if you own your own books.

5 *Take notes.* If you don't own your book, take notes as you read. Jot down main ideas in short, key phrases. Use outline or diagram form. When you're finished reading, go back over your notes to make sure you understand what you wrote and that you didn't forget to include an important point.

6 *Review your notes.* When you finish your reading, go over the main ideas in your notes or textbook. Close your textbook or notebook. Try to put the main ideas into your own words, out loud.

▶ **Writing It Out**

In many classes, you'll have to do written assignments. These assignments might involve working problems, filling in handouts, or writing out experiments. Here are some ways to stay on top of them.

7 *Read directions first.* Be sure you know what's expected of you before you begin. You don't want to get halfway through an assignment and realize you were supposed to use complete sentences when you've been writing in sentence fragments.

8 *Skim the assignment.* Decide which part of the assignment looks the hardest, and begin there. Save the easiest part until last.

9 *Break it into sections.* If it's an assignment that will take you a long time, do one section, and take a break. Then do the next section.

10 *Check your work.* Be sure you haven't missed anything. Is there a part you could do better? Is your work as neat as possible? Are all words spelled correctly?

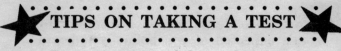

TIPS ON TAKING A TEST

Every once in a while teachers need to know if you've been paying attention. If you're like most people, thoughts of taking a test turn your stomach inside out. Relax! Here are some pointers that will help you keep your cool and do your best.

1 *Begin early.* If you know on Monday that you're going to have a test on Friday, study a little each day. Don't leave all your studying until Thursday night. Your brain can't absorb everything in one quick shot the night before a test. We learn best by studying in several sessions spread over a length of time.

2 *Know exactly what the test will cover.* If you don't know exactly what material will be covered on the test, ask your teacher. Don't waste time studying chapters that won't be on the test.

3 *Plan how you'll study each night.* Four days before the test, look over your textbook. Scan the headings for main ideas. Look at your underlined material. Three days before the test, review your notes. Highlight, circle, or underline key points. Two days before the test, start memorizing information. Refresh your memory the night before the test. If you have a chance, do a last-minute review during breakfast or on your lunch break the day of the test.

4 *Eat a good breakfast.* If you skip breakfast, your body's blood sugar never catches up the rest of the day. Without blood sugar, your brain goes blank.

5 *Get a good night's sleep.* Know how much sleep is best for you, and get it.

6 *Deal with test anxiety.* Try taking several deep breaths and exhale slowly and completely. Tell your body to relax all the way to the tips of your fingers and toes. Think positive thoughts. Tell yourself that you'll do fine—and believe it!

▶ Sitting Down to Take the Test

No matter what kind of test you're taking, the answers should be right at your fingertips. When the test is in front of you, you won't have time to sit and wonder what the answers are. One way to remember things is to associate them with a mental image, a sound, or a funny word. Another way is to use *acrostics*. Put things in a list, and make words out of their beginning letters.

Once you've got the test in front of you, be sure to read the directions first. Then look over the entire test to see what you're in for. Break the test into different sections, and decide how much time you can spend on each section. Don't forget to leave time to review your answers when you're finished.

When you get your test back, look it over carefully. Learn from what you did right and what you missed. Talk to your teacher about your work. She can help you see why you missed the questions you did. Always save your tests. Chances are, the next one will be similar.

RULES FOR BETTER WRITING

There's no way around it—being in school means writing papers. Most papers will fall into one of three categories. Either it's a research paper, a composition, or a book report. But all papers have some things in common.

All papers have three parts. There is a beginning, a middle, and an end. The beginning or topic sentence is where you state what you're paper will discuss. The topic sentence should capture the reader's attention. The middle or body is where you develop your topic. It may contain one or more paragraphs. The end is your conclusion. This is where you wrap up the ideas you developed in your paper.

Many times your teacher will give you a topic to write about. But sometimes it will be entirely up to you to choose a subject for your paper. Then what do you do? Try free associating to get your ideas rolling. Let your imagination go wild! Write down whatever comes to mind. After about five minutes, you'll have some great ideas!

IMAGINATION

When you have to write about a subject you know very little about, you need to research the subject. This calls for a trip to the library. To someone unfamiliar with a library, it may seem like a very confusing place. But the following tips can help you get the most out of your trip to the library.

1 *Ask the librarian.* The librarian is probably your most important source of information. If you have a question, just ask.

2 *The catalog can help.* Every book in the library is listed in some kind of catalog. Books can be listed in a card catalog with drawers full of 3 x 5 cards. They also can be listed on strips of film called microfiche. Or, books can be listed on a computer.

All information in a catalog is listed alphabetically. You can find books by looking up their titles, subjects, or authors. If the books are listed on a computer, ask your librarian to show you how to use it.

3 *The Reader's Guide to Periodical Literature* is another feature at the library. These are large green books that list magazine articles by topic only. Start with the book that has the most recent articles, and look up your topic. The librarian can help you find the magazines you need.

4 *Look in the encyclopedia.* Most libraries have several different encyclopedias. You can get a good overview of most topics in this valuable resource.

Once you've found the information you need, it's a good idea to take notes on it. Use 3 x 5 cards (one card for each idea), or write on regular-size sheets of paper. Don't try to read every book or article the library has on your subject. Select only the best.

To organize all your cards or sheets of paper, spread them out on a flat surface. Decide what information should come in the beginning, the middle, or near the end. Move your cards around to see which one fits where. Then number the cards in the order that seems best. From this order, write a rough outline. You can always change it if you need to.

Once you've organized your information this way, the actual writing isn't hard at all. Just let your words flow. And don't hesitate to change your outline if your paper seems to work better another way.

This first attempt at writing your paper can be quite sketchy. Leave big margins around the edge of the paper to add things later if you want. If you're using lined paper, write on every other line. Don't worry how messy things look at this stage in the process.

If you can type and know someone with a word processor, use it. A word processor makes writing easy. It lets you work with your topic as much as you want. You won't have to worry about making a mistake because you can easily change it.

After you've finished your first draft, make it better. Here are a few ways to improve any writing you do.

1 *Use strong verbs.* These put feeling into your writing. Weak verbs make it flat and uninteresting.

2 *Use concrete nouns.* Concrete nouns are specific, not vague. Nouns such as *things, stuff,* or *junk* are too general.

3 *Use the active voice.* "She swung the bat" is an example of the active voice. "The bat was swung by her" uses the passive voice. Many good writers use the active voice because it's much stronger.

4 *Avoid using too many adjectives and adverbs.* Your writing can benefit from a few well-chosen adjectives and adverbs. It becomes bogged down with too many.

5 *Avoid using clichés.* Clichés are overused phrases that you hear a million times every day. Some examples of clichés include "as good as gold," "clear as a bell," and "fit as a fiddle." Look for new and different ways to express your ideas.

6 *Check for neatness.* Whether you've handwritten your paper or typed it, be sure it's neat.

7 *Check your spelling and grammar.* There's no excuse for making a mistake in this area. Spelling and grammatical errors are the easiest mistakes to catch. Use a dictionary and your grammar book if necessary.

8 *Read your paper out loud.* This will help you decide if your paper sounds smooth.

3

We all look forward to spending time with our friends. It's a time to laugh and joke around and enjoy common interests. It's a time for sharing secrets and solving problems. Knowing how to make the most of this time is important.

A lot of the time you spend in school will be spent with friends at lunch, in class, and during activities. So, knowing how to get along with your friends is a skill you need to master to be successful in school.

Having good friends is great, but they can present some real challenges. For instance, what do you do when a friend asks you to lie for him? How do you deal with a friend who never returns the things she borrows? What about the friend who wants you all to herself? Being a friend and getting along with friends requires some specific skills. Master these skills, and you'll find success not only with friends, but also with just about anyone!

★ BEING YOURSELF WITH FRIENDS ★

Do you ever feel that you're not really being yourself when you're with your friends? If you hang around with a large crowd of friends, it's not unusual to feel this way. People can control the way we look, the way we act, even the way we think. Sometimes we live up to our friends' expectations because we want their approval. "Not me!" you might say. But ask yourself, "What would happen if I started dressing differently from my friends? Would they still be my friends if I disagreed with their views on dating or student rights?" Friends become friends because they enjoy being around each other and because they like the same things.

But sometimes, because you don't want to lose your friends, you may not be honest about the way you really think and feel. Maybe you pretend to be the way your friends would like you to be. But inside you feel angry and confused because you're not being honest with yourself.

How can you be yourself and still have a lot of friends? Here are some good ideas to get you started.

1 *Know yourself.* Stand in front of a mirror, and take a good look at yourself. What do you see? Notice your body dimensions, your facial features, the clothes you wear, and your hairstyle. Your outward appearance has a lot to do with who you are.

Now take a closer look at yourself. Who is the real person looking back at you? This may be a very hard question to answer. Your identity is made up of what you think, what you feel, and what you do.

The way you look at the world around you and what you think about it are unique to you. Your thoughts are your creation. Every day you form impressions of the people you meet, the sights you see, and the things you experience. Then your mind gives shape to these impressions. What you think is a part of who you are.

What you feel is part of your identity, too. We all experience many different feelings. But we don't all experience them in the same way. What are the things that make you happy, angry, or sad? Your emotional reaction to people and events in your life are part of your identity.

And finally, you are also what you do. Your actions are unique to you. Do you spend a lot of time studying, working in the yard, shooting baskets, or shopping? Do you run a mile every day, draw cartoons in your notebook, eat tuna fish sandwiches, or play the trombone? The combination of the things you do is unique to you.

So, as you're looking in the mirror, try putting all these pieces of yourself together. They make a total picture, and that picture is you!

2 *Like yourself.* So what if you don't fit the mold. You say that you're nose is too fat, that your legs are too short, or that your eyes are too small. So, you have too many freckles, too much hair on your arms, or not enough muscles. Or, maybe you think you're too sensitive or too quiet, or maybe too loud. Everyone has things that they'd love to change. But that's no reason to get down on yourself.

You're special. With all your unique physical, emotional, and intellectual qualities, you are one of a kind. Enjoy that feeling! Like who you are! That's the only way you'll really feel free to be you. Like yourself, and you'll feel happier. Like yourself, and you'll feel more alive, more interested in life, and more confident. Oh, yes—like yourself, and others will like you, too. And they'll want to be around you.

3 *Be yourself.* Once you've learned to like yourself, you might get to know parts of yourself that you never knew existed. These are the parts you've kept buried for the sake of pleasing others.

Maybe you think your friends wouldn't like you if they knew you listened to classical music. Maybe you think they'd make fun of you if you dressed the way you really would like to. These are risks you need to take.

Once you start really liking yourself, you won't feel the need for everyone's approval. The only person you need to please is you. So, let your secrets out of the bag! Be the person you really are. You may lose a few friends in the process, but you'll gain many more. People like being with people who know themselves, like themselves, and act themselves. Nobody enjoys a phony.

★ GETTING ALONG WITH FRIENDS ★

Sometimes it's tough to get along with friends. They may not be fair to you. They may become jealous of you. They may argue with you about everything. Sometimes maybe you'd just rather forget about them.

It helps to remember that friends are no different from anybody else in this world. Human beings are not perfect creatures. They have feelings that they often can't control and thoughts that they sometimes don't understand. They do things sometimes, without thinking how their actions affect others. As the saying goes, "You can't live with them, you can't live without them."

But there are ways to improve your friendships and make your time with friends more pleasant. Here are a few of them.

1 *Try to understand your friends.* Sometimes your friends may act in ways you don't understand. They may be impatient or grumpy. They may be unusually silly or silently depressed. Try to figure out why they're acting differently. Ask questions. Maybe your friend had an argument with her brother or sister. Maybe your friend is disappointed in a grade. Maybe she's just feeling lonely.

Don't automatically assume that you're the cause of your friend's unusual behavior. We all have moods that we can't seem to control. Sometimes knowing that a friend wants to help is the best medicine of all. But if your friend doesn't want your help, don't feel hurt. Some people just prefer to work out their problems alone. Give your friend some time and space.

2 *Accept your friends for who they are.* Don't try to change your friends. Maybe they don't dress as neatly as you do. Maybe they use perfume that you can't stand. Maybe they pop their gum! Hey, who wants to live with a bunch of clones? Let your friends be who they are. They'll enjoy being with you more, and you'll have more fun with them. As soon as people try to control each other, feelings get hurt, and tempers flare.

3 *Let your friends know how you feel.* Sometimes your friends *do* need to change the way they are, but they might not recognize this. They need to change their behavior when it infringes on your rights.

Suppose your best friend is always running late. She's never ready when you and your parents pick her up to go somewhere. If you spend a Saturday together, a lot of your time is wasted waiting for her to get dressed, fix her hair, or do a chore. You feel angry and frustrated.

Instead of letting these incidents pull your friendship apart, tell your friend how you feel. But wait until the incident is over and your anger has died down. Then gently tell her what she does, how it makes you feel, and explain why. You could say, "Sarah, it seems that whenever we plan to do something together, you're never ready on time. Sometimes

I've had to wait a couple of hours for you, and that really makes me angry. I don't enjoy sitting around waiting. I wish you could be ready when I arrive so we can have more time for fun."

If you speak honestly and openly, your friend will probably think about her actions. She may not have been aware of how you felt. You might even be able to discuss ways she can change her behavior.

4 *Know how to say no.* Sometimes your friends may ask you to do something you don't want to do. Because you don't want to lose them as friends, you agree. What can happen?

Suppose your friend asks you to lie for him. When the coach wants to know why he isn't at practice, you make up a story to account for his absence. You know he's really gone fishing with another friend. How will you feel when the coach finds out the truth? He's going to think that neither one of you can be trusted.

It's important to be honest about your feelings. And you need to be honest not only with other people, but also with yourself. Being honest about your feelings is saying "my feelings count." It takes a lot more courage to stand up for your feelings than it does to give in to other people's wishes. Rather than lie for your friend, you could say, "No, I don't like being dishonest. Telling a lie for you would make me feel very uncomfortable, and then people couldn't trust me."

Sure, your friend might get angry at you for a while. But in the long run, don't you think he'll respect your honesty. Now he knows that he can believe you. He knows you can be trusted. You should never feel bad about saying no. If you have strong feelings about something, you have the right to speak up.

 KEEPING YOUR FRIENDS

Once you've found a circle of friends, keep them. And this isn't difficult if you follow these suggestions.

1 *Be appreciative.* Let your friends know you appreciate them. Invite them over to your house for dinner or a slumber party. Throw a surprise party for your friend on her birthday. If you're going to the library, offer to return your friend's books. Help him out with homework. Offer to take class notes for him when he's absent.

2 *Be available.* This doesn't mean you have to spend every free minute with friends. But friendships need to be nourished. Schedule time to be with your friends or at least to call them on the phone. If your friend needs someone to talk to, try to make time for her. If you're too busy at the moment, let her know when you'll be free.

3 *Be faithful.* Nothing ends a friendship faster than unfaithfulness. Being faithful means keeping secrets you've promised to keep, not spreading vicious rumors, and not breaking commitments you've made. How would you feel if a friend spread rumors about you? Don't break that trust if you want to keep your friends.

4 *Be honest.* If you're upset about something your friend has done, let her know how you feel. Otherwise, your bad feelings will mushroom and won't ever be resolved. It's also important to be honest when your friend asks for your opinion about something. Even if you disagree, your friend will want to hear the truth.

★ MAKING NEW FRIENDS ★

If you've recently moved or changed schools, you may need some help making new friends. Sometimes it's hard to get started. You may feel unsure of yourself in new surroundings. Circles of friends are already well established, and you're wondering where you can fit in.

One good way to make new friends is by getting involved in extracurricular activities. You'll be more likely to meet someone with similar interests if you join a school club. Conversations spring up automatically if you're working on projects together, planning events, or discussing goals. As you work with others, you learn more about them. When the club meeting is over, offer a few friends a ride home. Maybe you can even plan a meeting at your house. Give other students a chance to know you better.

You could join a team. Whether it's a debating team, a chess team, a swim team, or a football team, teamwork brings people closer together. Don't be afraid to ask for advice or to offer it to someone else. Being a member of a team is a great way to get to know others and to help them get to know you.

If you're not very outgoing, here are a few tips on how to break the ice.

1 *Offer your help.* If you notice that someone needs help with homework or a club project, don't hesitate to step in. Simply ask if you can help. The rest will happen automatically.

2 *Ask for help.* If you don't understand something in or out of class, ask a reliable person for help. You'll know by his response if he's the kind of person you'd want for a friend.

3 *Give a compliment.* If you like what another student is wearing or how she performs on a team, let her know. She might be a person who needs someone else to take the initiative. Offering a compliment tells people you are friendly and outgoing.

4 *Agree with someone.* If you agree with a comment someone makes, let her know. She'll enjoy hearing someone agree with her. And the door will be open for more discussion.

5 *Find something in common.* Say, "You're wearing the same kind of shoes I am," or "Yeah, I loved that movie, too." People like being around others with similar tastes and interests as their own. If there's someone you want to get to know, look for something you have in common.

Once you've broken the ice, you're on your way to making a new friend. Think of ways to spend time together, like studying, having fun, eating lunch, or walking home. You might need to take the initiative for a while. Some people take longer than others to feel comfortable with a new friend. But the more you can share about yourself—your interests, your concerns, your goals—the sooner your friendship will become strong. Once you've opened up to a person, he'll feel safe about opening up to you. And before you know it, you'll have a new friend!

4

Soon after the school year begins each fall, so do the extracurricular activities. And it seems like there are tons of them to choose from. How are you ever going to choose between all the activities?

There are so many different sports.

There's football, soccer, hockey, lacrosse, track, basketball, swimming, baseball, tennis, golf, gymnastics and maybe even more at your school. Whew! Are you feeling confused? Try looking at the list of clubs. You'll probably find drama, chess, sewing, science, art, debate, and language clubs. And don't forget about special events committees to work on dances, assemblies, pep rallies, and fundraising. Are you feeling faint? You could always join student council for a little experience in government. There's the school newspaper, the yearbook, the radio station, or the literary magazine. Or, maybe you've got some musical talent and want to be a band, orchestra, or choir member.

"Stop! Stop!" Maybe you feel ready to quit before you even begin. But remember that life at school doesn't have to be all work and worry. When the final bell rings, there's also time for fun and for doing what you want. If it's relaxation you're after, you can find it. If it's greater knowledge and skill you're looking for, you won't be disappointed. And best of all, there's plenty of opportunity to be with friends and to make new ones.

If you've already decided that you don't want to head straight home after school, be sure you know how much of a commitment you can make. Once you join a team, a club, or a committee, you've committed a certain amount of your time and energy. Be sure you know how much time and energy is expected of you each week. And be sure you have that amount to give.

Before committing yourself to anything, you might want to make a schedule of what you have to do in a typical week. Be sure to include the time you spend in classes, studying at home, doing chores, being with friends, and relaxing. If you're involved with activities at church or with a youth group, account for that time, too. Then look at the time you have available. Is it enough time for the activity you're interested in? With practices and games, sports are probably the most time-consuming. But band, orchestra, and choir can keep you busy, too. Know what you're getting into. If it fits into your schedule, then go for it!

 DECIDING WHAT'S RIGHT FOR YOU

Choosing an extracurricular activity is like choosing anything else. You have to know what you're looking for. You wouldn't shop for clothes without knowing your size. Don't look for an extracurricular activity without knowing what you hope to gain from it.

Extracurricular activities are to stu-

dents what after-work activities are to parents. No one wants to work and be serious all the time. We all need opportunities to unwind, be ourselves, and have fun. That's why your parents join bridge groups, adult sports leagues, sewing and literary circles, health spas, and volunteer organizations. Extracurricular and after-work activities help round out our lives. They give our lives balance.

So, what will it take to give your life some balance? What activity will fill your personal needs? Below are some questions to ask yourself to help you make those decisions.

1 *Are you looking for athletic challenge?* Then consider a sport. There are lots to choose from. Think of what you enjoy and do best. If you like working with others to achieve a goal, try a team sport. If you're more of a loner, an individual sport may be better for you.

2 *Do you want to explore some career ideas?* Maybe you have thoughts of being an actor or actress, a professional athlete, a journalist, a government official, or a musician. There are extracurricular activities that can give you the experience you need.

3 *Do you enjoy being creative?* Maybe you have talents in art, drama, writing, or music. Opportunities to express yourself creatively make you feel good about yourself.

4 *Do you like helping others?* Some schools have service clubs that do volunteer work in hospitals and nursing homes. Your school may also need student tutors to help those having difficulty with schoolwork. Opportunities to try out your helping skills will teach you more about yourself. It may give you ideas for a future career as well.

5 *Are you good at planning activities?* Most schools have clubs and committees where you could shine. Dances, pep rallies, and all kinds of assemblies need to be planned. Student council often creates committees to work on specific tasks, like cleaning up the school grounds, raising money to buy new gym equipment, or solving the problem of school vandalism.

6 *Could you use extra practice with a school subject?* Try working on the school newspaper for lots of experience in writing. Or, for some math practice, see if there's a job running the cash register in the school cafeteria. Some schools have science clubs that make science lots of fun. And foreign language clubs will show you what it's like to live in Mexico, France, or Germany.

7 *Do you like intellectual competition?* Chess clubs and debate teams are popular everywhere. Contests in spelling, math, writing, music, and art are, too.

8 *Do you want to reduce stress?* Anything that provides you with exercise will help get rid of stress. Activities involving creative skills such as playing an instrument, drawing, painting, and sewing do, too.

Maybe now you're getting a clearer picture of the best extracurricular activities for you. You may even have a small list to choose from. The trick is narrowing it down.

Look at your schedule to see how much time you can devote to extracurricular activities. Then match this with the time each of the activities on your list will take. Your list should be getting smaller.

Number your last few choices in order of preference. If you're down to three or four activities, try to get more information about each one of them. Ask older students who might have tried the activities you're interested in. They can tell you things you wouldn't hear from anyone else. This information should help you make your choice.

At the beginning of the school year, there's a big temptation to rush into a lot of activities. Friends may try to talk you into joining different groups. Before you make any commitments, remember your answers to the above questions. Know what you're looking for in an extracurricular activity. Joining an activity just because your best friend is in it probably is not a good idea. And even if you don't know anybody in your new club, don't worry. There will be plenty of new people for you to get to know with similar interests.

SO YOU'RE NOT A STAR

It's easy to join activities with hopes of being a star. We all have dreams of getting standing ovations and cheers from the crowds. Wouldn't it be great to be the best pole vaulter, a champion chess player, or a piano virtuoso? But if you're joining a sport or activity just to gain the respect and admiration of your classmates, then think again. There's room for lots of disappointment.

What if you don't succeed at first or even ever? What if your goal of winning the admiration of others never comes true? Haven't you noticed that people who look to others to define their worth become easily discouraged?

Finding success with extracurricular activities doesn't mean being a star. It means having fun, being the best you can be, and enjoying the challenge. Don't worry about giving the crowds what they want. Concentrate on what *you* really want.

Do you want to be able to run a mile in six minutes, play *Moonlight Sonata* on the piano, increase your chess rating by 100 points, or do a jackknife off the high dive? Work at goals that are important to *you*. Challenge yourself. Test your limits. Feel good about every accomplishment.

It takes hard work and dedication to get where you want to be. Don't set your goals so high that you feel overwhelmed by them. Establish realistic step-by-step goals. And remember that you're never a loser until you give up trying.

Suppose you want to be able to swim a half mile. You can't expect this kind of performance without some preparation. Make a series of goals for yourself. The first two weeks you could work toward swimming 10 laps. Increase this goal by five laps every two weeks. At this rate, you'll be exactly where you want to be in three short months.

You'll be a star every day that you work toward your goal. You'll feel that fabulous sense of accomplishment that comes with hard work and dedication. Remember that you can't be really successful at something unless you enjoy it. You may not be the best outfielder or the best debater or the best flutist. But if you're having fun, you're finding success!

Your enjoyment may come from being around other people with similar interests. It may come from doing an activity that's a lot of fun. It may come from helping others, learning new skills, or being creative. No matter what activity you enjoy, if you're being the best you can be, you're a success!

★ GETTING ALONG ★
WITH A GROUP

Joining an extracurricular activity means joining a group. And that means you'll be in for some new experiences. Here are some things to think about.

1 *Don't make commitments you can't keep.* When you become a member of a group, you make certain commitments to that group. Whether you're joining a team, a club, or a committee, you're promising the other members some of your time and energy. And that fact cannot be taken lightly.

If you join a team, you're expected to come to all the practices and games. You're expected to perform to the best of your abilities. If you join the orchestra, you're expected to come to all the practices and performances. You need to practice your instrument because you have to contribute to the orchestra's overall performance. The contribution you make to a club is equally important, especially if you have a key role in the club.

People want to know they can count on you. Don't make a commitment to a group unless you know you can keep it. Not showing up for practices or club meetings will show the other members that you're not really a trustworthy member of the group.

2 *Be understanding of other group members.* Part of belonging to a group means trying to understand the actions and feelings of others. From time to time, we all need someone who will listen to our problems. When you sense that a fellow group member is feeling low, try to help out. You could say, "Dan, you've been missing a lot of practices lately. And when you're here, you just don't seem to be your old self. Is something bothering you? Can I help out somehow?"

3 *Be open to criticism.* Being a member of a group means being open to criticism by that group. If you're not performing up to group expectations, you'll probably hear about it.

Let's say you're supposed to make five posters for the pep club. If you show up with only two posters, they might say,

"What's the big idea? You said you'd make five posters and you only made two. Now someone has to do extra work. Do you want to be in this club or not? We need your support."

Sometimes we're not prepared for how angry others may feel toward us. Try to keep calm and look at the facts of the situation. Ask yourself if it really is your fault. Try to understand how your irresponsibility could make others angry. If you are to blame, apologize, and explain why you didn't keep your commitment. Offer to make up for it somehow. You could say, "I'm sorry. I didn't realize how busy I would be over the weekend. Maybe I could go to the art room during lunch and make three more posters. I really want to be in the pep club.

Next time I won't make a promise unless I'm sure I can keep it."

If you know ahead of time that you won't be able to contribute what's expected of you, then don't commit yourself. You could say, "I better not promise to make posters this weekend. I have a big test to study for and an English paper to write. Can someone else do it this time? I'll make extra posters for another pep rally."

4 *Speak up if you're unhappy about something.* There may be times when you feel you're being treated unfairly by another group member or even by the coach or club advisor. You may feel that you're expected to work harder than other group members or that you're given too much responsibility. Or, you may feel that your efforts are going unnoticed and someone else is getting all the credit. Don't keep your feelings bottled up inside. Speak up! You could say, "Coach, I've been coming to all the practices and working hard. My batting average is third highest on the team. But you never put me on the starting lineup. Is there something I'm doing wrong that I should know about?"

Without getting emotional, this team member states the facts as he sees them. The coach can probably sense his disappointment and confusion. Instead of getting rude and obnoxious, the player assumes the coach has good reasons for his actions. But the player doesn't hesitate to ask what those reasons are. He has a right to know.

It's always best to speak directly to the person you are unhappy with. Never criticize a person behind his back. And don't think about quitting an activity unless you've tried your best to solve the problem.

5 *Concentrate on doing your best and enjoying yourself.* As a member of a group, it's not unusual to feel the pressure of measuring up to the group's expectations. If you're not a fast enough runner, you'll lose points for the entire team. If you're not a good enough drummer, the whole band will suffer. Sure there may be room for improvement—and you'll want to improve. But don't pay too much attention to the judgment of others. Just concentrate on doing your best!

Some extracurricular activities demand more than others. If you're not a person who can cope with the pressures of group performance, maybe you'd be happier in an activity that is less demanding.

EXTRACURRICULAR ACTIVITIES

So, what's the formula for success with extracurricular activities? It contains seven major points.

→ 1. Know what you want.
→ 2. Make the best choice for yourself.
→ 3. Keep your commitments.
→ 4. Be the best you can be.
→ 5. Understand and help fulfill the needs of others.
→ 6. Speak up about your own needs.
→ 7. Enjoy yourself!

Extracurricular activities are meant to be enjoyed. They give you time to unwind and be yourself. They provide balance to weeks that may seem too heavy with work.

If you're considering participation in an after-school activity, make your choice wisely. Read back over the selection process in this chapter. Know what kind of commitment each choice requires. Then give it your all! Teams, clubs, and musical groups need people like you. They need your talent, your dedication, and your enthusiasm.

As a member of an activity group, your goal should be not only to do your best but also to help others do their best. There may be times when fellow team or club members need your support and encouragement. Remember that a group is made up of individuals just like you.

Finally, enjoy yourself! If you're not having fun, then try to figure out why. Is the time commitment too great? Is the activity too structured? Is the coach or advisor too strict? Are other members unfriendly? If there's someone you can speak to about your problem, do it. There may be a simple solution to your problem. But if you've tried and tried to work matters out and they just won't get better, think about a different extracurricular activity.

5

So far, you've learned how to find success with grades, with friends, and with extracurricular activities. But school success isn't achieving any *one* of these. You really need to succeed in all three areas to be a complete person.

True school success requires a careful balance of getting the grades you want, being with the friends you enjoy, and participating in extracurricular activities that meet your needs. It's like eating the right foods for good health. The nutritional balance you get by eating from all the basic food groups helps you feel your best. Just as a diet of only potato chips would make you feel pretty blah, so would a diet of nothing but books. We all need variety.

Think of it as a juggling act. You have to keep each of the three balls in the air. As one rises, another falls, and a third waits in line. Without letting your grades fall, you can participate in a sport or club and see your friends on the weekends. When you need to give attention to one area, the others have to wait. But you don't want to forget about them. Keep all three aspects of your school life moving.

Achieving this kind of balance is no easy trick. It requires knowing a lot about yourself and scheduling your time appropriately. Read on for some tips on how to be a great juggler.

 KNOW YOUR OWN LIMITS

It's so easy to get caught up in wanting to please everyone—your parents, your friends, your teachers, your coaches. This pleasing mentality often causes students to burn out. They begin feeling like a rat on a treadmill with no end in sight.

If all you do is try to please others, you'll soon begin to feel angry. If you want to find success in school, go after it for yourself. Do it because *you* want to be the best you can be. When you're self-motivated, you come alive inside.

To achieve the kind of balance that brings school success, it's important to know your own limits. How do you work best? What does it take to make you be the best you can be? Here are some specific questions to ask yourself.

1 *How much sleep do you need each night?* Most of us feel best when we get at least eight hours of sleep every night. If we get less sleep than this, we don't feel our best. Be sure not to shortchange yourself on sleep. If you do, something is going to suffer.

2 *How much time do you need to yourself?* Time by ourselves helps us sort through our feelings. If you've had a frustrating day, you may need more time by yourself than usual. Being alone with yourself may help you put things in perspective.

3 *How much time do you need for exercise?* You'll feel your best if you make time for regular exercise. Decide how much and what kind of exercise you prefer to do. Do exercise that fits in with your schedule.

4 *Do you need time with your family?* Sometimes it feels good to get away from your parents and brothers and sisters. But sometimes being with your family can be just what you need. When the responsibilities of your life seem overwhelming, it feels good to know you've got your family.

5 *How much time do you need for fun?* We all need time for fun, and most of us would like a lot more time than we get. But realistically speaking, how do you function best? Do you need 15 minutes of fun now and then throughout the day? Or, do you prefer waiting until the end of the day to get crazy? Maybe you need a period of fun right after school and then another before going to bed.

If you know you need time to yourself after school, then take it. If your homework comes easier when you take a music break every hour, do it! It's all a matter of recognizing your style and developing it.

It's easy to overextend yourself. You want to do it all and do it well. The only problem is that you can't, or you'll just get stressed out. No one has unlimited time and energy. We have to know our own limits, accept them, and work with them.

So, if you know that you have certain requirements each day, don't neglect them. If you need eight hours of sleep each night or an hour to yourself after school, make that a priority. There's no way you can be your best if you don't respect your needs.

SET PRIORITIES

We've talked about this before. But since it's so important to achieving balance, let's deal with it again. No one with a busy schedule ever survives without setting some priorities. Here are a few things you need to know to help you make sure your best energy will be spent in the right places.

1 *Know how much time you have to accomplish each task.* The shorter the time you have to do something, the higher its priority. If you have just a few hours to study for a test, then that should be priority number one. If you have a week to study for a test, then you can fit studying time around other activities. But as your test gets closer, your studying time will become more critical.

2 *Know which tasks require the most energy.* Some people are most alert and energetic in the evening. But many of us work best during the first several hours of the day. Do those tasks that require the most energy during your most productive time of day. Don't fritter away your best time and energy on unimportant tasks.

3 *Know which tasks you dislike the most.* It's pretty easy to postpone the tasks we dislike most. But if you do these tasks first, you'll feel a great sense of relief.

4 *Keep a daily list of tasks in order of priority.* Actually write out your list on a separate sheet of paper. Number each task. Then dig in!

5 *Cross out tasks as you complete them.* What a great feeling!

6 *Don't worry if you don't finish your list.* At least you accomplished the most important tasks. Put the tasks you didn't reach on the next day's list or even postpone them until you have extra time.

 BE MORE EFFICIENT

We all wish we could work faster than we do. But we are stuck with human brains and human bodies (aliens and androids not included!). We get tired and need rest. But one way to work faster is to learn to be more efficient. If your list of important tasks is longer than you can manage, think of ways to save time and energy. Here are a few more ideas.

1 *Learn how to use a word processor.* If you don't have a computer at home, see if your library has one for people to use. Learning to write papers at a word processor can save you hours!

2 *Hire someone to type or word process your papers.* If you're really in a crunch, this may be the way to go. You can spend your energy in other, more important ways.

3 *Ask a friend, brother, or sister to help you.* If you promise to repay the favor, somebody will probably help you out with a task. They might type your paper, hem a dress, or take the dog to the vet.

4 *Whenever possible, use teamwork.* If you have a big test coming up, try working with your friends. Each friend can take a different area to research.

5 *Divide your jobs into smaller units.* Sometimes it's easier to find an extra 15 minutes than it is to find a half hour. If you want to practice your flute for a half hour each day, try doing it in two 15-minute periods instead of all at once.

6 *School success doesn't always come from working harder.* It can come from working smarter. And if you learn to work smarter, you'll achieve more of the balance you're looking for.

 BATTLE STRESS

Sometimes it seems like your obligations just get to be overwhelming, and you start to neglect your own needs. You know where you're headed. Stress City, here you come! A certain amount of stress is good for us. It keeps us motivated. But when stress begins to affect the way we feel, our sleeping patterns, and the way we behave toward others, it's time to do something about it.

The pressures of school life can become too great at times. Setting priorities, knowing our limits, and becoming more efficient are all ways to minimize stress. Here are a few more tips to help you cope with stress.

1 *Take time out.* You're studying for a science test, but you can't remember the formulas. You're typing an English paper, and you just made five mistakes in one line. Take time out! Give your mind and body a rest. Stretch out on your bed. Take a walk outside. Turn on some music, and dance. Grab a snack. Call a friend. Do some jumping jacks. You'll feel refreshed and ready for work again soon.

2 *Say no.* You may be feeling stress because you committed too much of your time. You promised a friend you'd help her shop for a new dress. You offered to make extra favors for a party at a nursing home. You have good intentions, but make sure you have the time and energy to carry them out. Don't fill your daily list of things to do with more than you can handle. It's okay to say no when someone asks for your help. Just give a brief, honest explanation, and they'll probably understand. Much of the stress we experience is self-induced. Learning how to limit your obligations by saying no is a survival tactic.

3 *Think positive thoughts.* Start out your day by telling yourself what a great person you are. Feel confident about starting another day. Tell yourself that you'll be able to deal with whatever comes your way—and really believe it.

4 *Relax.* There are several good ways to relax your mind and body. One is to think of a special, very peaceful, and beautiful place you'd like to be. Take your mind there, and experience the scene with all of your senses. After a few minutes, return to the present, and go back to what you were doing.

Another way is to tell all the muscles in your body to relax. Start with your toes, and work up to your head. Move slowly, and don't forget a single inch.

A third way to relax is to tense muscles in your body and then relax them. Work with large muscle groups only, like your calves, thighs, and shoulders.

All of these relaxation techniques can be practiced right at your desk. Sit in a relaxed position. Close your eyes. And begin. If you can lie down on the floor or on a sofa or bed, you may be able to relax more easily.

If you've tried a

lot of the techniques in this chapter but are still feeling overwhelmed by the pressures in your life, talk with someone. A good place to turn is to your school counselor. He's trained to help you evaluate your situation more closely. And he may have suggestions you might not think of. It's comforting to know that you don't have to handle your problems alone.

Let your parents know how you're feeling, too. There may be ways they can help. Maybe they can relieve you of some chores or help you study for a test. If they know how you're feeling, they won't add more responsibilities to your list.

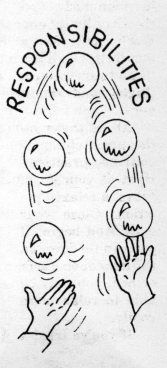

Now that you've had a few lessons on how to juggle your responsibilities, you need some practice. It's tough keeping all those balls in the air!

Achieving the kind of balance that's important to school success doesn't come overnight. Like anyone learning a new skill, you'll make some mistakes at first. You'll spend too much time decorating for a school dance and not get the grade you wanted on a math quiz. You'll knock yourself out writing an English paper and find out it wasn't due for another week. Don't expect perfection.

Eventually, with the advice in this book, you'll get better at learning how to pace yourself. You'll learn to recognize when you need to speed up or slow down, when to get involved or step aside.

So, don't be afraid! It's all out there waiting for you—the grades you want, the friends you need, and the extracurricular activities you enjoy. You can do it! School success can be yours! Go for it!